With

A Priest and Pastor's practical guide to
walking alongside God's work of
Recovery from Addiction

Rev. Marti Steiner Unger, RCP

ISBN-13: 979-8-9906735-5-7

Printed in the United States of America

This book is dedicated to all who have been, are, and will be brave enough to begin walking with God towards recovery from addiction.
You've got this!
You are beloved.
You belong.

It is also dedicated to Rev. Dr. John R. Unger II, my beloved husband and companion on this and every journey: thank you for your faith, patience, and laughter. May the God who knit our lives together bless every mile we've walked—and the adventure that lies ahead.

Forward

I am so grateful that you are doing research on how to be a good steward of your Christian faith as you walk with someone in recovery from addiction. Typically, our seminary training is woefully void of classes that offer real, transformative, practical guidance to faith leaders when it comes to addiction. And historically, the Church has not loved those struggling with addiction the way we have truly been called so to do. So, the fact that you are here with an open mind and ready to learn needs to be acknowledged; blessings to you!

Let's sit with the following data for a moment.

In 2023, 17.1% of people age 12+ in the U.S. had a substance use disorder in the past year.

That's about 1 in 6 Americans.
(Substance Abuse and Mental Health Services Administration)

That is a statistic for only substance use disorder. But there are many other ways people can struggle with addiction: gambling, sex, shopping, food, gaming, media (phones), etc. So, what do you think the real percentage of addiction might be in your own faith community? How many families sitting in your pews are impacted by addiction? And what can you, as their faith leader do about it? How can we walk with people towards healing and mended relationships?

As a priest in the Episcopal branch of the Jesus movement and as a Recovery Coach Professional who has personally trained and empowered thousands of Recovery Coaches, I have had the unique opportunity and honor to witness the incredible impact recovery from addiction has on people, families, churches and communities. It is a true blessing to witness people healing and relationships restored in real time.

And, I love people who struggle with addiction currently.

As clergy in the Christian faith, we are each called to bring people closer to God, by the way of love. How do we do that?

I'm glad you asked! Before we begin, please grab a cup of tea or coffee, quite your environment and prepare yourself by keeping an open mind ready to learn and an open heart ready to love. Let's begin by talking about how we live relationally.

Chapter One

Relationships

As Christians, we are called to relationship.

Our faith can be simply summed up in the following scripture:

> "Teacher, which commandment in the law is the greatest?" He said to him, "'You shall love the Lord your God with all your heart and with all your soul and with all your mind.' This is the greatest and first commandment. And a second is like it: 'You shall love your neighbor as yourself.' On these two commandments hang all the Law and the Prophets."
> (NRSVUE, Matt. 22.36–40)

Love God. Love your neighbor. Love yourself. That seems pretty simple, right?

Is it?

At its very core, love means relationship. In loving your neighbor, love is choosing presence over performance and people over projects. This love is something that, no matter how smart it becomes, AI will never replace. Love really isn't complicated, but it *is* costly—in our time, our attention, our resources, and in humility. Fortunately for us, God has already paid the price of love with His Son; we just bring our hearts.

As faith leaders, it helps to remember we're practicing relationships. Our role is to empower people as they grow into who God's calling them to be. Note the small but crucial vocabulary note: **empower** is *our* verb. "Fix" belongs to God

And let's be honest: the recipe for clergy burnout is trying to do *God's* job. Either we exhaust ourselves attempting to direct life overhauls we were never created to perform, or we are crushed under the expectation that we can.

Spoiler: we can't. Pastors who try to fix everyone end up like phone batteries at 3%—running hot, lots of warning notifications, and desperately seeking an outlet.

Sense you are reading this book, repeat after me (seriously- say it out loud with me):

I am not called to fix anyone!

Say it again. Say it one more time.

As a pastor or priest, you most likely have felt this urge to fix when parishioners meet with you about difficult issues they are dealing with. Faith leaders almost always come preloaded with the same hardware as ER nurses and those folks who can't ignore that crooked picture frame hanging on the wall: almost all of us have an inborn 'we've got to fix this problem right now' reflex. You spot a problem and something deep in your pastoral DNA leaps up like, "Stand back—I've got a bible verse, a whiteboard, a pot of coffee and a committee for backup!"

Now, this isn't coming from being prideful or a place of arrogance; it's a primal, inborn instinct. How many times when the emergency spotlight shines in the sky, you fling on your holy clergy cape and suddenly you're calculating solutions to the issue faster than the office photocopier can jam!

So, when a parishioner sits down across from you with a life messier than the church hall after a wedding, you will probably feel that familiar urge—the pastoral equivalent of reaching for band aids and duct tape (at least around here, those pretty much fix everything). Your heart means well: mend the break, heal the broken heart, and give order to the chaos (preferably before that second cup of coffee). Does this type of scenario sound familiar to you?

So, let's get serious and talk about how to approach relationship.

The Spectrum of Attitudes

In the *Technology of Prevention Workbook*, William A. Loftquist developed the three spectrums of attitudes—people viewed as objects, people viewed as recipients and people viewed as resources. Let's explore the meaning of the spectrum of attitudes, and how it is relevant to care in our context.

People Viewed as Objects – Do *TO*

This attitude is when a person or group of people "know what's best" for another person or group of people. The person or group of people does programs and activities TO another person or group of people (it is when we "should" on people: now, I said *should*: "You should do this", etc.).

Reflection: When were you treated as an object and how did you feel?

In our society, treating others and being treated as an object is the norm. Starting at young age with our caregivers, in school, at work (especially those in the military), with our friends and families, and even our own government treats us like objects (if you doubt that, try not paying your taxes and see what happens!). Think about a specific time when you have been treated like an object and were told to do something. Maybe your boss told you to how exactly to complete a project, a loved one gave you unsolicited advice, you had to stand in a long line at the DMV to renew your license, etc. What exactly happened and how did you feel at that moment?

For most people, the immediate reaction is one of feeling unworthy, feeling demeaned, unintelligent, or perhaps even a feeling rebellion emerges. Why?

Because as humans, we want to feel like we have agency over ourselves, that we belong, that we have value. When we are treated like an object, we feel like we are being treated as 'the other', as someone who is not a real part of the solution, but rather a tool to get the job done.

So, we know how it feels to be treated like an object. As clergy, we need to be mindful of this spectrum and work to reframe the way we relate to people: our goal is to treat people as the beloved resources God has called them to be.

People Viewed as Recipients – Do *FOR*

This attitude is when a person or group of people still believes they "know what's best for the other person or group of people, but they "give" them the opportunity in some decision making, thinking it will be "good" for them. The person or group of people does programs and activities FOR another person or group of people.

Reflection: When were you treated as a recipient and how did you feel?

An example of this might be if I hold up two pairs of pants and ask my son "Do you want to wear the blue pants or the brown pants?" This seems like a better option, a better way to treat people as I am giving my son a choice.

But who is still picking what pants he wears that day? I am. What if he really wants to wear green pants, or perhaps even shorts? Nope, that's not a choice. Although it seems like a better option, treating people like recipients still ignores their need for their own autonomy.

People Viewed as Resources – Do *WITH*

This attitude is when a person or group of people has respect for another person or group of people on what can be done. This attitude promotes self-esteem and productivity. The person or group of people does programs and activities *WITH* another person or group of people.

Reflection: When were you treated as a resource and how did you feel?

The attitude of WITH creates a community in which people are viewed, respected, and involved as resources and is the goal of every priest and pastor walking with people looking to overcome difficulties (with God's help) in their lives.

Our focus as faith leaders needs to be building relationships where people are treated as resources, knowing that they are valued as they are and able to overcome challenges they are facing. That is how we are called to love: by treating people as beloved people created in God's image. We aren't called to 'fix' people but rather *walk with* them as they are empowered to become who God calls them to be, to grow closer to God. This is our true calling as pastors and priests.

So, in a world where treating people like objects is pervasive, how do we give people agency and treat them like a resource in practice? I'm glad you asked! We will be discussing how we are "ABLE" (Advocate, Believe, Listen, Empower) to walk towards empowering people to move towards healing, restoration and who God calls them to be.

Chapter 2

ABLE

Advocacy

Therefore, as God's chosen ones, holy
and beloved, clothe yourselves with
compassion, kindness, humility,
meekness, and patience.

Colossians 3:12

You, as a faith leader, stand with people
at the crossroads of pain and possibility.
People bring us their most vulnerable
stories, and the way *we* name those
stories either opens doors toward help
and healing or quietly deadbolts them.
That's why advocacy, particularly
against stigma (and in our case,
especially the stigma surrounding
addiction)—is not some side mission to
think about; it's central to pastoral care,

congregational culture, and our public witness.

Stigma is not just a set of mean words or sideways glances; it is a *real* barrier between suffering people and the help they need. As the Centers for Disease Control and Prevention (CDC) notes, stigma includes "negative attitudes, beliefs, and stereotypes" and it "can prevent or delay people from seeking care or cause them to discontinue treatment." When our churches are rife with biases, absorb or worse, promote even a fraction of that stigma (and historically, we have), we unintentionally make healing much harder.

Addiction is a complex, chronic, and treatable health condition with spiritual, relational, and physiological dimensions. Yet many churches and people still frame it purely as a moral failing (sin) or a matter of willpower. We, as pastors, can *and need* to disrupt that narrative. We do this by telling the fuller truth about substance use disorders and the pathways to recovery. Stigma makes it difficult for people with substance use disorders to get help- a reality pastors see when congregants hide addiction, relapse or avoid support groups because they're afraid of being labeled.

Here's a short activity to illustrate stigma. I am going to share a sentence, and I'd like you to grab some paper and write down the first four descriptive things about the person I have described. Just immediately write down how you 'picture' this person- what are they doing, what do they look like, how they are behaving, etc. Here we go.

<u>My uncle is an alcoholic.</u>

Please write down the first four descriptive adjectives of how you envision my uncle.

How did you describe what my uncle looks like? What was he doing? How was he behaving?

The top adjectives that are commonly used in this thought experiment are:

abusive, lazy, drunk, messy, dirty, broke, and loud.

Some common words you have probably heard in your community (or have personally) used to describe people who struggle with an addiction are the following: addict, alcoholic, junkie, dirty/clean, bum, druggie, user, dealer, tweaker, abuser, crackhead, crackwhore, dopehead, methhead, pothead, drunk, psycho (and many more)…

Now, what if I told you that my uncle was a kind, soft-spoken loving husband and father, devout in his faith and never missed a day of work in his successful career. Yet, he still struggles with an alcohol addiction.

Is that what you envisioned? No.

So, why has stigmatic language become so common, so engrained in our families, communities and society? Why do groups of people use this language when describing people struggling with an issue (addiction, mental health, poverty, etc)?

Because it makes us feel better about ourselves. We aren't 'those people', we are better than them, we feel elevated. Stigmatic language has become normalized in our society, because it sets us apart.

So what does God have to say about this?

"Jesus told this parable to some who trusted in themselves that they were righteous and regarded others with contempt: "Two men went up to the temple to pray, one a Pharisee and the other a tax collector. The Pharisee, standing by himself, was praying thus,

`God, I thank you that I am not like other people: thieves, rogues, adulterers, or even like this tax collector. I fast twice a week; I give a tenth of all my income.' But the tax collector, standing far off, would not even look up to heaven, but was beating his breast and saying, `God, be merciful to me, a sinner!' I tell you, this man went down to his home justified rather than the other; for all who exalt themselves will be humbled, but all who humble themselves will be exalted." (Luke 18:9-14)

When we use stigmatic language, **we** are breaking our calling *towards* relationship.

That is the sinful power of stigma. Stigma strips people of their humanity: stigma defines and labels people as the difficulty they are struggling with. Stigma makes people feel shame over issues they didn't choose (I have *never* met anyone who *chose* to struggle with addiction); it undermines individual wellbeing and community health. When people are labeled or devalued, the consequences often span emotional, cognitive, and physical domains.

Individuals who experience stigma may withdraw from relationships, and most struggle with isolation, anxiety, or depressive symptoms. They may also avoid environments that should be supportive—such as workplaces, schools, and houses of worship—out of concern of judgment or public embarrassment: *it tragically often keeps them from reaching out for help completely*. Over time, this social pressure can erode mental health, elevate stress, disrupt sleep, and delay access to appropriate care.

Let's reflect: have you ever *personally known* someone you suspect struggled with some kind of addiction, but would not reach out for help because they didn't want to be judged? What happened to this person over time?

Were they able to find sobriety on their own, or did they silently struggle for years? If they had lived in an environment free of stigma, would they have reached out for help sooner?

As faith leaders, addressing stigma is both a pastoral responsibility and a formation priority. Our Christian faith calls us to honor every person as created in the image of God; stigma does the opposite by reducing a complex human life to a single label, which *never* illustrates the full humanity of anyone.

Left unchallenged, stigma discourages confession, silences prayer requests, and prevents families and individuals from receiving timely support. Teaching congregations to recognize and reject stigmatizing language and attitudes fosters a culture of honest disclosure, appropriate referral, and sustained care. In doing so, churches become safer, more compassionate communities—

places where dignity is upheld, health is promoted, and hope is put to action.

According to William White, our lives are greatly impacted by the words we use about ourselves and others. The words we choose to use to describe people can:

empower or disempower,
humanize or objectify,
engender compassion or elicit fear and hatred,
inspire us or deflate us,
comfort us or wound us,
bring us together or render us enemies.
(p. 2)

So what do we do? How can we help people 'CLEAR' stigma?

CLEAR Stigma

Here is an acronym to help us work together to 'CLEAR' stigma.

Compassion- Listen with an open heart. Nurture relationships by showing kindness and humility without judgement. Loop back what is shared for understanding.

Language- Most likely in the exercise prior, we saw examples of language that are not helpful to people who are stigmatized. How can we change our language to reduce stigma? How can we educate our church to use better language?

Use language that empowers people.

Empowerment- Explore and encourage the discovery of solutions to issues the person is dealing with. Don't tell them what to do, as we *do not know* exactly what they have experienced, nor do *we* know what a good pathway to betterment will be. Instead, help them discover their own path!

Affirmation- Encourage the person you are walking with: remind them they are made in God's image and loved as they are!

Respect- Be curious, present and demonstrate respect through your actions. Thank them for the opportunity to walk with them as they grow with God.

CLEARING stigma is important for all people…
it is how we put the human back into humanity.

When we counter stigma with language that promotes dignity, people are more likely to speak up early—before a crisis spirals into a catastrophe.

Language is one of our most powerful pastoral tools. The words we choose in daily conversations, in counseling, and when we are in front of our congregations can either reinforce shame or cultivate safety. Public health guidance is clear: person-first language reduces stigma. Use 'a person with a substance use disorder' in place of addict, alcoholic, etc. Use 'positive/negative' in place of (testing) 'clean/dirty' and the word 'sober' in place of clean (ex: my friend has been sober for three months).

Priests and pastors are culture-setters; when we model respectful, accurate language, teams, small groups, and prayer ministries follow suit. Over time, a congregation that talks about addiction with compassion will respond to it with compassion—shifting the atmosphere from suspicion and judgement toward a trusted community and support.

Advocacy against stigma also means making the church a real on-ramp to care. People are more likely to seek treatment when the first disclosure is met with empathy, confidentiality, and a clear path forward.

That path might include peer-led recovery groups, faith-compatible programs, warm referrals and connection to clinicians, and ongoing support for families who are navigating exhaustion, boundaries, and the grief that comes with addiction. This isn't about "outsourcing" pastoral care; it's enlarging it.

There's another reason this advocacy belongs to pastors and priests: stigma wounds the *whole* body of Christ. When people feel they must hide what they are struggling with, the church loses their gifts and their story of grace-in-progress. When we replace stigma with hospitality, those stories come to the surface and discipleship deepens.

Recovery practices—rigorous honesty, confession, amends, daily interdependence—are profoundly aligned with Christian formation. As the church learns to accompany people through messy, typically non-linear healing, we discover again that sanctification is a community project.

Pastoral advocacy also carries into the world: our communities wrestle with overdose, incarceration, family fracture, and homelessness—all of these threads are often tied to untreated substance use disorders and mental health issues. Faith leaders can help connect to a wider recovery community, convene coalitions, and bless and support recovery-friendly employers. We are committed to loving our neighbor and moral clarity.

By walking with those in recovery, we choose practices that honor each person's God-given dignity. When we reject stigma and shame, we open the door to real help—getting people into care and supporting them long enough for healing to take root. This is how our church bears Christ's mercy: by listening without judgment, walking alongside, and persevering in love.

Finally, pushing back against stigma protects pastors and congregations from burnout and cynicism. Shame-driven cultures breed secrecy, crises, and compassion fatigue. Where have we seen this in the Christian church historically? Did perpetuating stigma bring people closer to God?

By contrast, stigma-aware churches practice sustainable care: they set healthy boundaries, they normalize seeking help, and celebrate small steps—first appointments kept, milestones reached, honest conversations had, relapses faced with renewed plans and restored relationship and support. This is slow, but it is sacred work. Every time a person takes one more step toward recovery because your church felt safe, you have participated in the ministry of our calling towards reconciliation.

As priests and pastors, we are a steward of words, spaces, and expectations. We use that trust to dismantle stigma and honor the dignity of those God loves. We speak truthfully, listen deeply, and bless every honest step toward help. In doing so, we do more than remove a needless barrier to care—we bear credible witness to Christ, who came "to bind up the brokenhearted" and to set captives free.

Chapter 3

A<u>B</u>LE

<u>Believe</u>

"Now faith is the assurance of things hoped for, the conviction of things not seen. Indeed, by faith our ancestors received approval. By faith we understand that the worlds were prepared by the word of God, so that what is seen was made from things that are not visible."

(Hebrews 11. 1-3)

Do you *really* believe people can change?

Now I'm not talking about the tidy, well-rehearsed "yes," but the embodied *yes* that reshapes our personal framework, our prayers, the very way we live. The *yes* that fills us with *hope* when someone sits across from us and says, "I messed up again."

If the gospel means anything, it means this: no human story is finished while the God of grace is in relationship with us. We are ministers of a kingdom where tombs crack and air fills lungs that were still. Where death is no more, and eternal life is given to us. Where addiction and shame do not get the final say.

Every person who crosses our path bears the image of God. This isn't something we've earned: the imago Dei is the first word God speaks and breathes into every life and the last truth that stands when all the labels and stigma fall away.

Think about people you personally know that society deems "the other": the housing challenged woman living in her car, the man holding a sign asking for assistance at the corner by the gas station, the people going in and out of the recovery house or a MAT (Medically Assisted Treatment) clinic, the single parent paying for groceries with a government assistance card, the person walking out of the correctional facility, having served their time.

When you see these people in your community, do you hear the Spirit whisper: "This is a beloved, made in the image of God?"

This is not soft theology. It is the bedrock of who Jesus calls us to be.

"For by grace you have been saved through faith, and this is not your own doing; it is the gift of God— not the result of works, so that no one may boast. For we are what he has made us, created in Christ Jesus for good works, which God prepared beforehand so that we may walk in them." (Ephesians 2, 8-10)

Our belief in grace is the river running over that bedrock. Grace is not a pat on the head or a pass on accountability. Grace is the living, flowing power of God to raise the dead. Grace doesn't say, "It's fine." Grace says, "You are mine," and then rearranges our lives to make room for love. Grace forgives and then teaches hands to do work that is good, trains lips to tell the truth and puts feet on a path towards relationships rooted in love. Grace is the presence of Jesus: Jesus who sits down and eats with the 'wrong' people. Jesus who interrupts the stoning. Jesus, who calms the waters. Jesus, who lays hands on people struggling with the stigma of leprosy, those whom the "righteous" keep outside.

So what does it mean to believe— to *really believe*—that people can change?

It means we let God's grace move through both us and the person in recovery with help of the Holy Spirit. We

find a night of the week and light a
candle and say, "This is where we listen,
tell the truth, pray, and begin again."
We spend time and build relationships—
the addiction counselor who will take a
call, the intake specialist who will meet
someone at noon, the peer mentor who
will drive across town at 11 p.m. We put
helping phone numbers on speed dial,
not in some binder gathering dust on a
shelf. We budget for rides to treatment,
for training our ushers in trauma-aware
hospitality, for safe policies that protect
children and to dignify those in early
recovery.

It means we practice compassion. We
ask, "what happened?" and say, "we will
walk with you" and "who is the person
God is calling you to be, and who are
the people and resources you need to
get there?" and "You belong and are
loved."

It means we proclaim forgiveness as
more than God's kindness; we proclaim

it as *grace into brokenness that once owned each of us*. We bless those in recovery as part of the church's normal life. Because God's table is for the hungry, not the perfect (after all, church is where *we all* find healing and restoration, including us as faith leaders).

And it means we give our congregations something to do with their hope. A casserole for a sober house. A note in the mail to someone in week two of recovery. A prayer group that names names (with permission), day after day. Training so our greeters know how to welcome all with open hearts. A shared testimony so the people can *hear grace in a human voice and see the image of God shine through*.

The measure of our ministry is not how many people never stumble again; it is whether you and God's people in your care keep embodying the mercy of Jesus in a world that has very little patience. Our job is not to guarantee outcomes, but to point people to God.

Our job is to be so infused with grace and so convinced of people reflecting the image of God, that the prodigal children *know* the road home and that *we keep watch for them*. Our job is the way *we run when we see them in the distance*, and by the way we *set the table in celebration* of restored relationships.

Simply put, as priests, pastors and faith leaders, *we believe people can change because they bear the image of God* and *because grace is stronger than death.*

And that faith in hope of God's grace and love is the most important thing we do when walking with people towards recovery. We need to be able to look the person in the eye and say "I know you can do this" and *completely believe it.*

Chapter 4

ABLE

Listen

You must understand this, my beloved
brothers and sisters: let everyone be
quick to listen, slow to speak, slow to
anger,

(James 1:19)

To be heard is to be dignified. For
someone in recovery, being honestly
listened to may be the first taste of
safety after years of secrecy, shame,
and misunderstanding. When a person
tells their story and finds you attentive,
unhurried, and unafraid, they begin to
believe that change is possible and that
they are *not alone* in the process. This is
why the imago Dei matters so much in
pastoral care: if each person bears
God's image, then their story is not a
problem to fix but a life to honor. As we

listen, we are bearing witness to the holy, helping them put words around pain and hope, and joining the Spirit in the slow work of healing.

People don't care how much you know, until they know how much you care. The way we listen announces what we believe about God and about them.

Active listening is the ability to focus completely on the person sharing, to try to understand where they are coming from, to comprehend their feelings, and to respond thoughtfully. It is not passive, nor is it a performance. It is disciplined attention—your whole self, turned toward the other, with judgment set aside and curiosity awakened. In pastoral care, active listening becomes a ministry of presence: you are not rushing to solve or to preach, but to make room for the person's truth to emerge. When we listen actively, we are saying with our posture and our words, "I see you. I'm with you. Your story matters." In recovery, where shame often chokes the voice and fear expects rejection, this kind of listening is medicine. It builds connection and mutual trust and helps the person in recovery identify what they need and discover next steps that fit their reality, not our assumptions.

Active listeners use both verbal and non-verbal ways to show empathy and keep attention on the one who is speaking. Start with empathy. Let your first words communicate that you are with them inside their experience. You might say, "I am so sorry you're carrying this. Thank you for trusting me with it. Let's figure out together what support could help." Empathy does not mean you agree with every choice; it means you are willing to feel with them. Empathy opens the door to trust, and trust is the doorway through which truth can walk.

As they continue, practice paraphrasing, looping back—brief summaries in your own words that show you are tracking their meaning and give them a chance to clarify. "So what I'm hearing is that the afternoons are hardest, especially when you're alone, and that yesterday you reached for the pills because you felt cornered and ashamed. Did I get that right?" Paraphrasing proves understanding and invites correction. It slows the conversation to the speed of care, stopping you from racing ahead to solutions they didn't ask for. Often, when people hear their own words reflected back with care, they find new language for what is happening inside them; sometimes they even correct themselves, catching a pattern they had not seen.

Invite them deeper with open-ended questions that cannot be answered with a simple yes or no. "I hear what you're saying about how church can feel overwhelming right now—can you tell me more about what parts feel safest and what parts feel hardest?" or "What changes would you most want to see in the next two weeks, and what would make those changes feel possible?"

Open questions hand them the pen to write down next steps; *they are the experts on their own story*. Follow this with gentle probing (open ended, motivational interviewing questions) when details matter: "When you say afternoons are a trigger, what typically happens around 3 p.m.?" or "Tell me more about the conversation with your sister—what was said just before you left?" Probing isn't interrogation; it is curiosity in relation to care, helping them explore specifics that help them discern supports and actions.

Sprinkle the conversation with short, sincere verbal affirmations that keep focus with them and let them know you are receiving what they're offering. "I

can understand why you feel that way."
"That makes sense." "I see." "Thank you
for saying that out loud." These simple
phrases are like steadying hands on the
railing as they navigate a steep
stairway. They don't redirect; they
reassure. Be mindful that your
affirmations are non-judgmental and
proportionate; they are not evaluations
("That's great!") so much as
acknowledgments that encourage
continued honesty.

Non-verbal listening matters just as
much, sometimes more. Your body
teaches as powerfully as your words. Sit
at the same eye level as the person
sharing; if they are on a couch, take the
chair nearby, not the desk across the
room. Keep distractions out of sight: put
your phone away, silence notifications,
move papers aside. Maintain natural
eye contact—not a creepy stare, but a
steady presence that says you are with
them. Nodding gently as they speak

affirms understanding without signaling agreement with every detail. A small, warm smile at appropriate moments can diffuse tension and communicate welcome, especially at the beginning or end of a heavy conversation. Avoid restless movements—glancing at your watch or the clock, tapping a pen, sighing, or scanning the hallway. Those micro-signals can make them feel like a burden. Your stillness becomes a sanctuary in which their words can settle.

The context you create also deepens listening. Choose a space that respects privacy and safety; nothing undermines trust like being overheard in a hallway. Begin with a brief orienting line: "I'm here to listen. We can think about next steps at the end if you want. How does that sound?" Structure helps support emotional safety. If you need to explain limits to confidentiality (for instance, in cases where someone is in danger, or as a mandated reporter), do so clearly and compassionately at the start. Boundaries are not the opposite of grace; they are how grace keeps people safe. Within those boundaries, let them lead the pace.

Reflective listening means I don't just *assume* I got your point: I say it back in my own words and ask, "Did I get that right?" That little loop (reflect → confirm → refine) turns vague understanding into real understanding and, just as importantly, it allows both of you feel accepted and safe enough to lower your guard.

Think of the classic "telephone" game: one person whispers, "I'm feeling overwhelmed at work," and by the time it reaches the last person, it's somehow become, "I'm feeding an elk at church" (which depending on where you live might be true, but that wasn't the original message!)

This is funny in a circle of kids; but not truly understanding is not so funny in pastoral care. We all *think* we heard the original message, but without summarizing and checking, the final version becomes distorted. By pausing to paraphrase—"So I hear that afternoons at work are toughest, and you're carrying a lot of anxiety—did I get that right?"—and letting the speaker correct or clarify, we keep the message from mutating, build trust, and invite deeper, more honest conversation.

As the sharing person's story unfolds, resist the urge to fix (say it with me again "I am not called to fix anyone!"). People in recovery often carry a lifetime of advice that didn't fit, solutions imposed without listening and advice that doesn't work for them. Instead of jumping to a plan, help them notice strengths and resources they already possess. "You've gone two afternoons this week without using—that tells me you've already started practicing something that works. What helped?" or "I heard you say your cousin texts at 4 p.m.—how might you lean on that support more consistently?" Listening in this way helps the person discover their own agency.

Recovery is not something we do to people; it is a path we walk *with them.*

Listening also includes truth-telling, but specifically truth-telling that arises from trust and is seasoned with grace. When appropriate, name concerns gently and invite reflection. "I noticed that when we spoke about the argument with your mom, your shoulders tensed and your voice got quiet. What's happening in your body right now?" or "You've said you want to stop drinking, and you've also said you keep liquor in the house for guests. How do those two things fit together?" These observations are invitations, not a way to impose judgement. They keep the conversation anchored in reality without shaming the person who is already vulnerable.

At the end of a conversation, summarize what you heard and ask what would feel most helpful next. "From what you've shared, afternoons and loneliness are key triggers; being outside and texting your cousin has helped; and Sundays are both meaningful and exhausting. What actions would support you?" When possible, make a small, concrete plan together and put it in writing or a quick text before they leave. Follow-through is a form of listening; it tells them you remember and you care.

All the while, keep holding the theological core: this person is an image-bearer, and *grace is real* (thank you God, alleluia!). Let that conviction shape your tone and your patience. Recovery is often nonlinear. When relapse happens, listening helps transform the moment from a verdict into *a learning conversation*. "Thank you for telling me. What did you notice in the hours before? What did the first impulse feel like in your body? What do you want to try differently if those same cues show up this week?"

Compassion does not cancel consequences, but it refuses to reduce a person to their worst moment. When people are heard after a relapse—without shock, without contempt—they begin to hope that their future is larger than their failure.

Listening, finally, is something you cannot offer sustainably unless you also receive it. Pastors and faith leaders need places where they are heard—colleagues, supervisors, spiritual directors, therapists—so that your own grief and frustration do not harden into cynicism. Protect time for rest. Pray honestly. Bring your tired heart to Jesus and to trusted friends and colleagues. The tenderness you extend to others must be tended in you. Your capacity to hear stories is enlarged when your own story is met with care.

This is the work: to sit beside saints-in-progress and sinners-beloved (which is to say, *all of us*), to look into eyes clouded by shame and embody with your presence before you say with your words, "I see you. I'm here. God is here." Then to listen—actively, attentively, with empathy; to paraphrase and clarify; to ask open-ended and gentle probing questions; to offer short affirmations; to nod and smile and stay still; to put your phone away; to keep your eyes and your heart where they belong; to help them name what is true and imagine what is next. Over time, these small acts become sacraments of hope. They knit trust, open paths to practical help, and make space for the Spirit to do what only the Spirit can do: renew minds, reorder desires, and raise dead places to life.

God and his grace will do the heavy lifting. Your listening makes room for grace to be felt. In that space, people discover that they are not their addiction; they are God's beloved, made in the very image of God. And because that is true, change is possible. So, keep the chair ready, the phone silenced, the lamp on. When they begin to speak, let heaven hear the quiet liturgy of your attention. In Christ, it is enough to begin—and beginning again is how lives and souls are saved.

Chapter 5

ABL**E**

Empowerment

So if the Son makes you free, you will
be free indeed.

(John 8:36)

I am not called to fix anyone.
I am ***not called*** to fix anyone.
I am not called to ***fix anyone***!

I know we've discussed this, but do you
personally struggle with trying to fix
people (and most priests and pastors
do, you are not alone)? Well, you
bought this book so there is a high
probability that you lean in that direction.

I have great news for you! Our God is a
gracious God and because Jesus died
for our sins, you don't have to!

As members of the Jesus movement, we talk a lot about love—loving God, loving our neighbor, and, with a surprising amount of awkwardness, loving ourselves. Jesus didn't offer those as three optional theological electives; He braided them together into one great relational commandment.

Love of God pulls us toward worship and wonder. Love of neighbor moves us toward service and solidarity. Love of self keeps us honest, humble, and human. When we walk with people in recovery, that threefold call becomes our compass. It tells us who we are, how to show up. It teaches us that empowerment is relational, patient, and practical. And it reminds us that while we can walk with people as they discern what resources they need, *we are not the resource*. <u>God is the Source</u>; we're the connectors.

First, our love for God sets the tone. When we say "God is the healer," we're not making some polite theological statement to open a meeting; we're confessing the truth that steadies all we do. We worship a God who notices sparrows and counts hairs—which means God notices relapses, rejoicings, and the Tuesday-afternoon blahs.

That kind of loving attention is the baseline of empowerment. Because if God is paying attention, we as faith leaders can relax our grip. We don't have to be the savior (thankfully, that position is filled). We are free to be the Church: a people formed by grace, steadfast with hope, and slow to panic. Love for God keeps us from confusing our role with God's role. It loosens the anxious voice of the world that whispers, "Fix this now or you've failed."

Love for neighbor is where empowerment takes on skin. It means we meet people as people, *not problems*. We learn names and stories. We honor boundaries. We choose good language and drop labels that flatten a whole human into a single struggle. We practice hospitality that doesn't look sideways with suspicion at folks but instead greets them like a beloved brother at a family reunion. In recovery work, love for neighbor sounds like, "What kind of support are you looking for today?" and "I'm here for the long haul," and "You are beloved and belong."

And love for self? That one often is like the dull paper cutter that gets stuffed behind the dusty filing cabinet. But Jesus includes it for a reason. Empowerment requires self-awareness and self-compassion. We cannot accompany people well if we treat our own bodies and souls like something disposable. Loving ourselves looks like setting boundaries that protect the relationship: "I can talk for twenty minutes tonight and again on Thursday." It looks like telling the truth about our limits: "I don't know the answer, but let's figure out how to find someone who does." It looks like taking rest seriously, because nothing says "I trust God" like honoring sabbath. When we love ourselves rightly, we show our neighbors what healthy love looks like—steady, present, and sustainable.

Now, let's talk about time—and about who carries the load. Simply, the person in recovery and God do the work. We don't. Consider this: do *we* actually know the right path to recovery for the person in front of us? We might have some idea because of biases we have, but we do not know what the right path to recovery is for the person sitting across from us. As priests and pastors, we are called love: to walk along with- but we don't take the steps for them. That sacred effort towards change belongs to the one in recovery, and to the God who meets them in the hard places and leads them forward.

For most people, this work with God takes time. Change learns to breathe before it learns to run. Progress often looks slow: one meeting attended, one honest phone call made, one boundary kept when no one was watching. Some days it's a single brave decision at 2:17 p.m. That's real labor—soul-and-body labor—and we honor it. We don't try to fast-forward and shortchange the process or carry what isn't ours to carry (because we can't anyway- *resist this fixing urge*). Instead, we offer presence, prayer, and empower connection to resources, trusting that strength grows in the person as they practice their change.

Our question isn't, "Did everything change this week?" but, "Are you facing the right direction, and how can we keep walking with you?" We acknowledge the bravery of moving towards change and show up with patience. So, we refuse hurry. We bear witness. We keep pace with our brother and sister who is doing the work, and we trust God the healer who is always faithful to finish what He starts.

Because empowerment takes time, we commit to being connectors rather than becoming the resource. There's a big difference between being helpful and being the hub of someone's life. The moment we become the hub (the fixer)—indispensable and constantly spinning—we've accidentally traded empowerment for dependency, and eventually, resentment.

Our call is to help people build their own network, not become their network.

Think of us as holy air-traffic control: we don't fly the planes, but we help connect them to those who can. Empowerment says, "I believe you can do this, and together, we are going to discover the resources you need, so you have a runway, some lights, and a crew." This dignifies people. It tells the truth that *they and God do the work*, and we watch their plane take off towards a sky of new life in God's calling.

Of course, being connectors requires humility. We have to admit what we don't know and find the people who do. That's not failure—that's love for God (who gifts the Body with diverse members), love for neighbor (who deserves the best help), and love for self (which says we aren't called to clone ourselves into fourteen professions).

And siblings in Christ, that is a relief! There's freedom in saying, "I'm the pastor; I'm good at sacraments, sermons, and showing up. For budgeting, let's call Leah. For legal advice, let's ring Bill. For trauma-informed counseling, who might be a good fit for you?"

Empowerment trusts the Body of Christ and the broader community.

Empowerment shaped by the great commandment also reframes accountability.

Because empowerment is relational, we invest in community. The opposite of addiction isn't sobriety—it's connection (Hari). We build small, ordinary bridges where connections take root: potlucks, support groups, choir practice, service projects, corporate worship, and the weekly ritual of stacking chairs after fellowship. Ordinary is where belonging takes root. Over time, those routines can create purpose. When a hard night comes, a person doesn't fall into the void; they fall into a web of names, numbers, and casseroles. That's love of neighbor in action with sleeves rolled up.

Let's also say out loud that setbacks happen. Not because people are weak, but because recovery is complex and life keeps throwing curveballs. Empowerment doesn't collapse into despair or devolve into drama. We keep perspective: "A set back is not the whole story, it's a learning point."

We revisit the plan. We reconnect to resources. We remind ourselves—and the person we are walking with—that God's mercy is renewed with the sunrise each morning, because God knows we live one day at a time.

And then there's the quiet miracle of self-empowerment we get to witness. *They* know the number to call. *They* know what meetings work and how to connect with them. *They* know how to pray with someone through a tough hour. You see their plan take hold, and *they* know what next steps are.

That's when you see the great commandment rippling outward: loved by God, a person learns to love themselves, and then they love others, and community. Love multiplied by mercy and grace.

A quick word about metrics. Churches love attendance counts and budget lines. Those matter, but empowerment asks for different measurements, many of them delightfully uncountable. Did we keep showing up? Did we refuse stigma and honor dignity? Did we walk with someone as they discovered the connection to what they needed? Did we model the great commandment in our tone, timing, and choices? If the answer is yes, then we are standing on holy ground.

So, what does empowerment look like in practice? We can keep it simple:

- **Love God:** Worship, pray, breathe. Remember who does the healing.

- **Love our neighbor:** Listen with reflection, ask good open-ended questions, use words that build God's kingdom on earth, believe people can change, show up, and invest time.

- **Love ourselves:** Rest, set boundaries, ask for help. We aren't called to become the resource; we need to remain open, encouraging, empowering connectors.

Empowerment becomes more than a strategy—it becomes our way of being. We honor the image of God in every person. We refuse to treat anyone as a project that needs fixed. We truly believe people can change and tell them. We give time the chance to do its slow, sacred work. And we celebrate that the same God who calls us to love is already loving, already healing, already moving ahead of us.

We reflect God's love.

We don't fix a life. We don't become the resource. We love God, we love our neighbor, we love ourselves, and we help empower people to grow closer to God, so grace can do what grace does best: heal, restore, and set people free.

God is good, all the time.
All the time, God is good!
Pray, Listen, Love, Repeat

Are you ready to feel more confident and grounded when someone turns to you in pain? **Listening with Love** is a transformational, one day online training that helps you develop the spiritual strength and practical skills to care with calm, clarity, and compassion.

Details and registration:
www.RootedinFaith.Love.

Acknowledgements

Centers for Disease Control and Prevention. "Examples of Non-Stigmatizing Language and Alternatives." *CDC Overdose Prevention*, Centers for Disease Control and Prevention, n.d., [URL].

—. "Mental Health Stigma." *CDC*, 9 June 2025, [URL].

—. "Stigma: Beyond the Numbers." *Stop Overdose*, 31 Jan. 2025, [URL].

—. "Stigma Reduction." *Stop Overdose*, 2 Apr. 2024, [URL].

Hari, Johann. "Everything You Think You Know About Addiction Is Wrong." *YouTube*, uploaded by TED, July 2015, www.youtube.com/watch?v=PY9DcIMGxMs.

Lofquist, William A. *The Technology of Prevention Workbook: A Leadership Development Program*. Associates for Youth Development, 1989, pp. 47–50.

New Revised Standard Version Updated Edition. National Council of the Churches of Christ in the United States of America, 2021. (Permission note— "Used by permission. All rights reserved worldwide."—is optional and usually not included in the Works Cited.)

Substance Abuse and Mental Health Services Administration. *Highlights for the 2023 National Survey on Drug Use and Health*. SAMHSA, 2024, https://www.samhsa.gov/data/sites/defa ult/files/NSDUH%202023%20Annual%2 0Release/2023-nsduh-main-highlights.pdf. Accessed 11 Nov. 2025.

White, William L. "The Rhetoric of Recovery Advocacy: An Essay on the Power of Language." *William White Papers*, n.d., http://www.williamwhitepapers.com/pr/2 001RhetoricofRecoveryAdvocacy.pdf. Accessed 30 Dec. 2020.

Thank you and may
God bless you always!

Revs. Unger

Bring the Rev's Unger
to your next event!

Whether you're planning a conference,
retreat, workshop, or special service,
Rev's Unger is available for dynamic
speaking and engaging facilitation.

To inquire or book now, email:
RevsUnger@Gmail.com

9 798990 673557